for the love of **SAN FRANCISCO**

Jim Brick

Jennie Brick

SCENIC NATURAL COOKBOOK

Photographs by Jim Brick

Recipes by Jennie Brick

© Visual Impressions Publishing 1994

All rights reserved. No part of this publication may be reproduced, stored in a retrieval system, or transmitted in any form or by any means, electronic, mechanical, photocopying, recording or otherwise, without prior written permission of Visual Impressions.

All photographs in this book are available as stock photographs and display prints. Contact Visual Impressions directly.

Visual Impressions Publishing
820 Sweetbay Drive
Sunnyvale, CA 94086, USA
tel: 408-296-1629
fax: 408-244-3172

All photographs were taken with a Leica-R camera, Leica lenses from 15mm through 350mm, and the Leica 2x Apo-Extender. Films used were Fujichrome Velvia and Fujichrome 100 Professional.

Jim Brick received his photographic education at Brooks Institute of Photography in Santa Barbara, California.

ISBN 1-878525-02-6
Printed in Hong Kong.

9 8 7 6 5 4 3 2 1

Introduction

This book came about because of our love for San Francisco. San Francisco is a very unique and beautiful city. Perched on a hill and surrounded on three sides by water. "The City by the Bay." Two gorgeous bridges, the Golden Gate and the Bay Bridge. And a song that truely says it all... "I left my heart in San Francisco".

Typically, scenic books of tourist areas are simply that, scenic picture books. Buy it. Look at it. Put it on the bookshelf and forget it. Could a scenic book also be a useful book? We think so. How about a cookbook... Cookbooks are very useful. Everyone likes to try new recipes. You keep cookbooks handy because there is at least one recipe in every cookbook that you really like. If that recipe happens to be in a scenic cookbook, think of the memories brought back when you look for the recipe and see the pictures. This book won't be lost on a forgotten bookshelf. It will be nearby whether you want to look at the pictures or prepare one of the recipes.

Just because this is a natural cookbook doesn't mean sacrifices have been made. The low fat, low cholesterol, high fiber recipes in this book are good. Every recipe has been taste-tested and approved by numerous friends and relatives.

This cookbook is a companion of "for the love of SAN FRANCISCO, a SCENIC ADDRESS BOOK". The address book contains thirty beautiful scenic views of San Francisco alternating with address book pages, note pages, and special information pages.

Jim & Jennie Brick

Pasta with Scallops and Shrimp

1 lb linguini or spaghetti
2 tbs olive oil
3 cloves garlic, minced
⅛ tsp red pepper flakes
1 lb sea scallops, halved crosswise
1 lb medium sized shrimp, cleaned
2 tbs chopped fresh basil
7 cups coarsley chopped fresh spinach
3 tomatoes, diced
2 tsp grated lemon peel
1 tsp salt
⅛ tsp pepper

YIELD: 6 servings

Cook pasta. Over medium high heat, heat oil in a large skillet or wok. Add garlic and red pepper flakes. Cook, stirring, for ½ minute. Add scallops, shrimp, and basil. Cook, stirring, about 2 minutes, until shrimp starts to turn pink. Add the rest of the ingredients and cook until spinach wilts, about 2 minutes. Toss with pasta in a warm serving bowl.

Variation: Serve over brown rice instead of pasta, or substitute pieces of well drained firm tofu for scallops and shrimp.

Sunrise over San Francisco and the Golden Gate Bridge.

Tuna or Tofu Sandwiches

YIELD: 4 servings

2 6 oz cans albacore tuna or 1 lb firm tofu, well drained
2 green onions and tops, sliced thin
½ cup toasted, slivered almonds
¼ cup mango chutney, chopped
2 tbs mayonnaise
salt and pepper to taste
8 slices whole wheat bread
lettuce or alfalfa sprouts

Mash tofu or tuna. Mix in onions, almonds, chutney, mayonnaise, salt, and pepper. Make four sandwiches, adding lettuce or alfalfa sprouts.

Sunrise over San Francisco and over Point Bonita, the entrance to San Francisco Bay.

Apricot Squares

2 cups chopped dried apricots
¾ cup water
½ cup oil
1 cup honey
3 egg whites
½ tsp almond extract
1 tsp grated lemon peel
2½ cups whole wheat pastry flour
2 tsp baking powder
1 cup slivered almonds

BAKE: 350°
TIME: 25-30 minutes
YIELD: 24 squares

Place apricots and water in a 2 qt saucepan. Simmer apricots for 5 minutes. Do not drain. Set aside. Mix oil and honey together. Add egg whites and beat until creamy. Mix in almond extract and lemon peel. Stir flour and baking powder together, then mix into honey mixture. Stir in almonds and apricots. Pour into greased 9x13 inch pan. Bake until toothpick inserted in center comes out clean. Cool in pan on wire rack. Cut into 2 inch squares.

Coit Tower and the Transamerica Building rise above San Francisco.

Cinnamon-Nut Coffee Cake

½ cup oil
¾ cup honey
3 egg whites
1 cup plain nonfat yogurt
1 tsp vanilla
2 cups whole wheat pastry flour
½ tsp salt
1 tsp baking powder
1 tsp soda

Topping:
¾ cup date "sugar"
1 tsp cinnamon
1 cup chopped walnuts, almonds, or pecans

BAKE: 350°
TIME: 35-45 minutes
YIELD: 8-10 servings

Mix topping ingredients together and set aside. Mix oil and honey together. Add egg whites and beat until creamy. Mix in yogurt and vanilla. Mix flour, salt, baking powder, and soda together. Add to yogurt mixture and blend. Pour half of batter into greased 9 inch spring form pan or tube pan and sprinkle with half of topping. Put rest of batter in pan and sprinkle with remaining half of topping. Bake until a toothpick inserted in the center of the cake comes out clean. Cover the cake with aluminum foil the last 10 minutes of baking if it's getting too brown.

The famous San Francisco Victorians.

Oven "French Fries"

BAKE: 425°
YIELD: 6 Servings

6 potatoes
oil

Scrub potatoes, then cut into "french fry" size pieces. Dry with paper towels. Pour 1 tbs oil in a bowl. Add the potatoes and toss to coat. Add a little more oil if needed. Spread potatoes on 2 baking sheets. Bake for 10 minutes, stir, and bake 10 minutes more, or until browned. Serve immediately.

A healthier alternative to deep frying, and just as good.

The Embarcadero at night from the waterfront.

Almond-Poppy Seed Muffins

BAKE: 375°
TIME: 20 minutes
YIELD: 18 muffins

2 ¾ cups whole wheat pastry flour
4 tsp baking powder
½ tsp soda
½ tsp salt
1 cup raw almonds, ground in blender
¼ cup poppy seeds
3 egg whites, beaten slightly
1 tsp almond extract
1 ½ cups nonfat or soy milk
¼ cup oil
¾ cup honey

Mix the dry ingredients in a bowl. Mix the liquid ingredients in another bowl. Combine dry and liquid mixtures, stirring only enough to moisten. Fill oiled muffin cups ⅔ full. Bake until muffins are firm in the center.

Things to see and do in Golden Gate Park.

Brown Rice - Wheat Pilaf

YIELD: 6-8 servings

¼ cup whole wheat berries
2 cups water
1 tbs oil
6 cups cooked brown rice, chilled (2 cups uncooked)
2 green onions, including tops, chopped
½ cup fresh parsley, chopped

Place wheat berries and 2 cups of water in a 2 qt saucepan. Bring to a boil. Reduce heat, cover and simmer for 1 hour and 15 minutes. Drain. Heat oil in skillet. Add rice, wheat berries, onions, and parsley. Heat, stirring often, until hot.

The Palace of Fine Arts at night.

"Hot Dog" Hash

YIELD: 6 servings

2 tbs oil
6 medium potatoes, baked, chilled, and cut in a ½ inch dice
½ cup chopped onion
9 tofu hot dogs, cut in ½ inch diagonal pieces
1 16 oz can corn, drained
2 tsp chili powder
1 tsp salt
⅛ tsp pepper

Heat oil in skillet. Add potato, onions, and tofu dogs. Cook over medium heat, stirring often, until browned. Stir in corn, chili powder, salt, and pepper. Heat through.

This is a favorite with kids as well as adults.

The Palace of Fine Arts is a great place for school outings.

Raspberry Almond Bars

1 cup whole, raw almonds
1 cup rolled oats
1 cup whole wheat pastry flour
¼ tsp salt
¼ cup oil
½ cup honey
1 tsp almond extract
1 cup all fruit raspberry preserves
½ cup sliced almonds

BAKE: 350°
TIME: 25-30 minutes
YIELD: 27 bars

Grind whole almonds in a food processor or blender. Put in a mixing bowl. Grind oats to a fine flour. Add to ground almonds. Stir in flour and salt. Combine oil, honey, and extract in a small bowl. Add to dry ingredients and mix well. Pat into a 9 x 13 inch pan. Spread preserves over batter. Sprinkle sliced almonds over top. Bake until lightly browned around edges. Cool in pan. Cut into 1x2 inch bars.

Can be mixed completely in a food processor. Grind almonds first, then add oats, flour, and salt. Process. Add oil, honey, and extract. Process until well mixed.

World renowned street artist George Allen Durkee, and picturesque Union Street.

Almond Rice

YIELD: 6 servings

1 tbs olive oil
4 cups cooked brown rice, chilled (1 ⅓ cups uncooked)
1 cup toasted slivered almonds
2 green onions, with tops, finely chopped
dash garlic powder

Over medium heat, in a 10 inch skillet, heat olive oil. Stir in rice, almonds, onions, and garlic powder. Heat, stirring often, until hot.

The entrance to Chinatown.

Curry Rice Salad

1 lb firm tofu, well drained
3 cups cooked brown rice, well chilled (1 cup uncooked)
3 tomatoes, chopped
1 cup raisins
salt
pepper

Dressing:
¼ cup olive oil
¼ cup lemon juice
5 tsp curry powder

Mix dressing, set aside. Cut tofu into ½ inch cubes. Place cubes on lightly oiled cookie sheets. Bake at 400° F, stirring cubes every 5 minutes until they are firm and slightly crisp. Mix tofu, rice, tomatoes, and raisins in a bowl. Pour dressing over rice mixture. Add salt and pepper to taste. Stir well and chill at least 1 hour. Serve with chutney.

YIELD: 6 servings

Even better the second day!

A view of Chinatown's busy streets.

Date Bars

½ cup oil
½ cup honey
½ cup orange juice
2 tsp grated orange rind
1 tsp vanilla
3 egg whites
2 cups whole wheat pastry flour
1 tsp baking soda
2 cups finely chopped dates
1 cup chopped pecans, cashews, or almonds

BAKE: 350°
TIME: 25 minutes
YIELD: 27 bars

Mix oil, honey, orange juice, orange rind, and vanilla. Add egg whites, beat well. Mix flour and soda together. Add to liquid mixture. Blend well. Add dates and nuts. Stir. Pour into an oiled 9 x 13 inch pan. Bake until lightly browned and firm in center. Cool completely, then cut into 1x2 inch bars.

Filbert Street (a stairway and gardens) and Napier Lane (a wooden walkway) is a unique San Francisco intersection.

Granola Bread

3 cups whole wheat flour
¼ cup gluten flour
1 tbs dry yeast
1 ¼ cups water
¼ cup honey

1 tsp salt
2 tbs oil
2 egg whites
1 ½ cups fat-free granola
1 ½ cups raisins

BAKE: 325°
TIME: 35 minutes
YIELD: 2 loaves

In large mixer bowl, combine 2 cups of the whole wheat flour, gluten flour, and yeast. In a saucepan or microwave, heat together water, honey, salt and oil to 115° F. Add to dry mixture in mixer bowl. Mix. Add egg whites. Beat ½ minute at low speed of electric mixer. Scrape sides of bowl. Beat 3 minutes at high speed. By hand, stir in remaining flour, granola and raisins. Place dough in 2 greased loaf pans, or one bundt pan. Cover with damp dish towel. Let rise in warm place until almost doubled, about one hour. Bake for 20 minutes, cover with foil, and bake 15 minutes more. Cool on racks.

Great toasted!

Ghirardelli Square (an old chocolate factory converted to shops) at night.

Country Bean Soup

YIELD: 2 quarts

¼ cup black beans
¼ cup kidney beans
¼ cup azuki beans
¼ cup pinto beans
¼ cup lentils
¼ cup small white beans
¼ cup baby lima beans
¼ cup green split peas
¼ cup yellow split peas

¼ cup whole dried peas
1½ quarts water
1 onion, chopped
1 cloves garlic, minced
1 28 oz cans crushed tomatoes
½ tsp oregano
¾ tsp basil
¾ tsp salt
⅛ tsp pepper

Wash beans. Place in a 4 qt pan. Add water until it's a few inches above the beans. Soak overnight. Drain and rinse beans. Put beans back in pan with 1½ quarts water, onion, and garlic. Simmer for 2 hours. Add tomatoes, oregano, basil, salt, and pepper. Simmer for 30 minutes more. If too thick, add a little more water.

Even better the next day!

The Japanese Tea Garden in Golden Gate Park, and the Carousel on Pier 39.

Caramelcorn

YIELD: 16 cups

¾ cup sunflower seeds
¾ cup unpopped corn
¾ cup honey
¼ cup blackstrap molasses

Toast sunflower seeds by placing in a pan over medium heat, stirring often, until toasted. Pop the corn. Remove all unpopped kernels. Place in a large bowl. Pour honey and molasses into a 2 qt saucepan. Bring to a boil. Boil until mixture reaches 265° F hard ball stage on candy thermometer, or until a small amount dropped into a cup of cold water forms a firm ball. Stir in sunflower seeds. Pour over popcorn. Stir to coat. Spread on waxed paper to cool. Store in an airtight container.

Pier 39 view with Coit Tower and the Transamerica Building in the background.

Crab Cakes

YIELD: 10 patties

1 lb crab meat
3 cups fresh whole wheat bread crumbs
4 egg whites
½ cup milk
¼ tsp pepper
2 tbs finely minced onion
2 tbs lemon juice
oil

Chop crab meat into small pieces. A food processor works well. Mix crab and bread crumbs in a large bowl. Beat egg whites slightly in a small bowl, stir in milk, pepper, onion, and lemon juice. Add to crab mixture and mix well. Form into patties and fry in pan brushed with a small amount of oil. Cook 4 to 5 minutes per side until golden brown.

Imitation crab may be used if you can find one with all natural ingredients.

Good in pocket bread with tomatoes and sprouts or served with potatoes, vegetables, and salad.

The San Francisco Waterfront from Pier 39 to Fisherman's Wharf.

Tasty Fish Cakes

YIELD: 4 servings

2 medium potatoes
1 lb cod fillets
½ tsp salt
⅛ tsp pepper
pinch of garlic powder
2 tbs minced parsley
oil for frying

Peel potatoes. Cut into quarters. Boil in enough water to cover, until tender. Drain. In a 12 inch skillet, place fish and 1 cup of water. Bring to a boil. Reduce heat, cover and simmer 5-10 minutes until fish flakes easily. Drain fish. In a medium sized bowl, mash potato and fish until well blended. Mix in salt, pepper, garlic powder, and parsley. Shape mixture into 8 patties. Cook patties in a small amount of oil in a skillet over medium heat 4-5 minutes per side, until browned. Serve with lemon wedges.

The San Francisco Marathon starts on the Golden Gate Bridge.

Fruit and Nut Snacks

½ cup wheat germ
⅓ cup soy flour
½ cup dry milk powder
½ cup oat bran
¼ cup honey
½ cup apple juice
2 tbs oil
1 cup chopped almonds
½ cup chopped walnuts
½ cup chopped cashews
1 cup raisins, chopped dates or chopped dried apricots

Mix wheat germ, soy flour, dry milk powder, and oat bran together. Mix in honey, apple juice, and oil. Stir in nuts and fruit. Mix well. Spread evenly in an oiled 8x8 inch pan. Bake until firm. Cut into 16 squares, but leave in the pan until cooled.

BAKE: 300°
TIME: 30-40 minutes
YIELD: 16 pieces

Good as a high energy snack food for skiing, biking, hiking, etc.

The San Francisco Marathon heading toward the Transamerica Building, and kite flying on the Marina Green.

Tuna Tortilla Casserole

2 medium onions, chopped
2 cloves garlic, minced
1 tbs oil
1 28 oz can crushed tomatoes
2½ tsp cumin
1 4 oz can chopped green chilis
2 cups sliced black olives
3 6½ oz cans tuna, drained
2 cups grated cheddar or soy cheese
12 corn tortillas, cut in sixths

BAKE: 350°
TIME: 30 minutes
YIELD: 6-8 servings

Saute onion and garlic in oil until soft. Stir in tomatoes, cumin, chilis, and olives. Simmer, covered, for 20 minutes. Stir in tuna. Spread 1 cup tuna mixture in a 9 x13 inch glass dish. Lay half of the tortillas in dish. Spoon half of tuna mixture over tortillas. Sprinkle on one half of cheese. Cover with the remaining tortillas. Spoon the rest of the tuna mixture over the tortillas. Top with remaining cheese. Bake.

The Golden Gate Bridge and Fort Point.

Seed Bread

6 cups water heated to 115° F
⅓ cup olive oil
⅓ cup honey
2 tbs salt
1 ½ cups gluten flour
14 cups whole wheat flour (approximately)

2 tbs yeast
3 cups oat bran
1 cup sesame seeds
2 cups sunflower seeds
3 cups raisins (optional)

BAKE: 350°
TIME: 35 minutes
YIELD: 4 loaves

Put water, oil, honey, salt, gluten flour, and 5 cups of whole wheat flour in large mixing bowl. Beat until smooth. Add yeast, beat for 2 minutes. You can use an electric mixer until this point, but unless you have a mixer designed to knead bread, you need to switch to hand mixing. Add 3 cups of flour, 1 cup at a time, mixing between each addition. Add the oat bran the same way. Add the seeds and raisins. Keep mixing and adding flour until the dough is no longer sticky, but don't add so much that the dough becomes dry. Put on a floured board and knead for at least 10 minutes. Place dough in a large oiled bowl. Turn over to grease top. Cover with a damp dish towel. Let rise in a warm place, (about 85° F), until almost doubled. Punch down, cut dough into 4 equal pieces. Form each piece into a loaf and put in greased loaf pans. Cover with damp dish towel and let rise until almost doubled. Bake until nicely browned.

Makes good toast.
Freeze extra loaves.

Fort Point protected San Francisco from attack by sea.

Yummy Eggplant

3 large eggplants
olive oil
2 15 oz cans tomato sauce
½ tsp salt
1 ½ tsp cumin
1 large garlic clove, minced
1 cup sliced green onion
½ lb mushrooms, sliced
1 6 oz can black olives, sliced
2 ½ cups shredded cheese- Monterey Jack, or soy mozarella

Slice the unpeeled eggplants into ½ inch thick rounds. Place slices on baking sheets and brush with oil. Turn over and brush other side. Bake in 450° oven for 20 minutes. Remove eggplant from oven and lower oven temperature to 350°. Meanwhile, place tomato sauce, salt, cumin, garlic, green onions, mushrooms, and olives in a 2 qt saucepan. Bring to a boil. Simmer sauce for 20 minutes. Place one layer of eggplant in each of two 8 ½ x 11 inch glass dishes. Top with sauce and cheese. Add another layer of eggplant, sauce and cheese. Bake until sauce is bubbly and cheese is melted.

BAKE: 350°
TIME: 20 minutes
YIELD: 6 servings

Views of San Francisco from above.

Apple Crisp

BAKE: 350°
TIME: 35 minutes
YIELD: 8-10 servings

6 large apples, peeled and thinly sliced
1 cup whole wheat pastry flour
1 ½ cups rolled oats
½ cup oat bran
½ cup date "sugar"
1 cup chopped raw almonds
½ tsp ginger
½ tsp nutmeg
½ tsp allspice
1 tsp cinnamon
¼ cup oil
½ cup honey
¾ cup raisins or chopped dates

Spread apples evenly in a glass 9x13 inch baking dish. Put flour, oats, oat bran, date sugar, almonds, and spices into a bowl and mix. Add oil and honey and mix well. You may have to use your fingers to get it evenly mixed into a crumbly texture. Stir in raisins or dates. Spread mixture over apples. Bake until golden brown.

Good warm or cold.

Try with nonfat frozen yogurt.

San Francisco and the Golden Gate Bridge from the Marin Headlands.

Basil Carrots

TIME: 12-15 minutes
YIELD: 6 servings

1 tsp oil
6 medium carrots, thinly sliced diagonally
½ tsp dried basil, crushed

Pour oil into 10 inch skillet, add carrots. Sprinkle with basil. Stir. Cover skillet and simmer until carrots are tender.

The Great Highway runs along Ocean Beach toward Lands End and the entrance to San Francisco Bay.

Holiday Cookies

⅔ cup oil
1 cup honey
3 egg whites
2 tsp almond extract
5½ cups whole wheat pastry flour
2 tsp baking soda

BAKE: 375°
TIME: 8-10 minutes
YIELD: 5 dozen
             2 inch cookies

Mix oil, honey, egg whites, and extract thoroughly. Mix flour and baking soda together. Blend in.

Roll dough on a floured board to ⅛ inch thick. Cut into shapes with cookie cutters. Place on oiled cookie sheets. Bake until lightly browned. Cool on racks.

Variation: Use vanilla in place of almond extract.

The San Francisco - Oakland Bay Bridge at sunset from Yerba Buena Island.

Honey-Mustard Tempeh

TIME: 25 minutes
YIELD: 4 servings

1 lb tempeh
½ cup honey
¼ cup dijon mustard
½ tsp salt
1 tsp curry powder

Cut tempeh into ½ inch pieces. In small pan, over medium heat, stir honey, mustard, salt, and curry powder until well mixed. Place tempeh in a shallow baking dish. Pour honey-mustard mixture over tempeh. Turn tempeh to coat with sauce. Cover dish and bake.

Good served with brown rice, carrots, broccoli, and a green salad.

A view down San Francisco's Market Street from Twin Peaks Overlook.

Whole Wheat Biscuits

2 cups whole wheat flour
3 tsp baking powder
¾ tsp salt
⅓ cup oil
⅔ cup nonfat or soy milk

BAKE: 450°
TIME: 10-12 minutes
YIELD: 12 biscuits

Mix flour, baking powder, and salt in a bowl. Pour oil and milk into flour mixture. Mix well, then place on a floured board. Knead a few times. Roll out ½ inch thick. Cut with biscuit cutter. Bake on cookie sheet.

Very different flavored and textured biscuits can be made by using different flours. Try pastry flour, hard wheat flour, or a combination of both to find the one you like the best.

Animals at the San Francisco Zoo pose for the photographer.

Vegetable Pot Pie

1 medium cauliflower, cut into florets
3 carrots, sliced into ½ inch chunks
½ lb green beans cut into 1 inch pieces
2 large red potatoes cut into 1 inch chunks
1¼ cups water
1½ cups peas, fresh or frozen
1 12 oz can corn, drained
3 tbs olive oil
1 medium onion, finely chopped
2 cloves garlic, minced
3 tbs whole wheat flour
½ cup vegetable cooking water
1½ cups nonfat or soy milk
2 tsp tamari sauce
⅛ tsp pepper
2 tbs chopped parsley
1½ cups cooked beans
2x biscuit recipe (previous page)

BAKE: 425º
TIME: 20-25 minutes
YIELD: 6-8 servings

Cook cauliflower, carrots, green beans, and potato in water until tender. Just before they are done, add the peas and corn. Drain, reserving the cooking liquid. Saute the onion and garlic in oil for about 3 minutes until onion is soft. Add flour and cook 1 minute more. Add ½ cup vegetable cooking water and stir. Add the milk and cook, stirring constantly, until sauce thickens. Add tamari sauce and pepper. Stir the vegetables, parsley, and beans into the sauce. Put vegetable mixture in a 9x13 inch glass pan. Roll biscuit dough into a rectangle, ½ inch thick. Place dough over vegetables. Trim around edge of dish with a sharp knife. Cut a few slits in dough to let steam escape. Place dish on baking sheet. Bake until browned.

A cable car pulling up the Hyde Street Hill.

Apple Muffins

½ cup oil
½ cup honey
3 egg whites
1 cup nonfat or soy milk
1 tsp grated lemon peel
2 ½ cups whole wheat pastry flour
4 tsp baking powder
2 tsp cinnamon
1 cup shredded, unpeeled apple
½ cup sunflower seeds

Beat together the oil and honey. Add the egg whites, milk, and lemon peel. Beat until well blended. Blend the flour, baking powder, and cinnamon. Add flour mixture, apple, and seeds to creamed mixture all at once. Stir just until blended. Fill oiled muffin cups about ⅔ full. Bake until lightly browned.

Variation: Add a half cup raisins or chopped dates

BAKE: 375°
TIME: 20 minutes
YIELD: 18 muffins

The Powell Street Cable Car Turnaround.

Barley-Mushroom Soup

YIELD: 4-6 servings

8 cups water
1 lb mushrooms, sliced
1 medium onion, chopped
1 cup pearl barley
⅓ cup tamari
1 clove garlic, minced
¾ tsp basil
⅛ tsp pepper

Bring all ingredients to a boil in a 5 qt saucepan. Reduce heat, cover, and simmer for 1 hour and 30 minutes or until barley is tender.

Variation: Add 1 tbs sherry after soup is cooked.

Free concert every Sunday at Stern Grove.

Rhubarb Cake

2 tbs oil
½ cup date "sugar"
½ cup chopped pecans or almonds
¼ cup whole wheat pastry flour
1 tsp cinnamon
2 ½ cups whole wheat pastry flour
1 tsp baking powder
1 tsp soda

1 tsp cinnamon
½ cup oil
¾ cup honey
3 egg whites
1 cup nonfat yogurt
1 tsp vanilla
2 ½ cups chopped rhubarb

BAKE: 350º
TIME: 30-40 minutes
YIELD: 12 pieces

Mix the first five ingredients in a small bowl. Set aside. This is the topping. Mix flour, baking powder, soda, and cinnamon together in another bowl, set aside. In a large bowl, beat together the oil, honey and egg whites until light. Mix in yogurt and vanilla, then flour mixture. Stir in rhubarb. Pour into a greased 9x13 inch pan. Sprinkle topping over batter. Bake until toothpick inserted in center comes out clean.

Good served warm or cold.

Lombard Street, the "crookedest street in the world", and Coit Tower.

A few helpful hints....

Use a mixture of ½ liquid lecithin and ½ peanut oil to grease baking pans. Use a pastry brush to apply. This is a healthier alternative to solid shortening or butter.

When measuring oil and honey for a recipe, measure the oil first. This will coat the measuring jug and the honey will slip right out.

All unfamiliar sounding ingredients should be available at your local health food store.

...Jennie Brick